All His Breakable Things

poems by

Jiordan Castle

Finishing Line Press
Georgetown, Kentucky

All His Breakable Things

ACKNOWLEDGMENTS

My immense appreciation and gratitude to the following journals, in which
versions of these poems first appeared:

Vinyl for "Barbed Wire"
Third Point Press for "The One Where _____ _____"
Verdad for "The MetroCard Machine Asks Whether I Want to Add Value or
      Time"
Frontera for "Handheld"
Cagibi for "Disappearing Act"

Thank you to Catherine Barnett, Donna Masini, Grace Schulman, and Tom
Sleigh for their guidance and support; to all the wonderful friends who gave
time and attention to many of these poems; to my family for their generosity
of spirit; and always—to Jerrod Morgan and our dog, Hacksaw, for their
unwavering faith in me.

Publisher: Leah Maines
Editor: Christen Kincaid
Cover Art: Jaya Nicely
Author Photo: Jenna Breiter
Cover Design: Elizabeth Maines McCleavy

Printed in the USA on acid-free paper.
Order online: www.finishinglinepress.com
      also available on amazon.com

Author inquiries and mail orders:
Finishing Line Press
P. O. Box 1626
Georgetown, Kentucky 40324
U. S. A.

Table of Contents

For my family

Barbed Wire

to keep people in,
      out,   birds off.
In winter,
pigeon has to settle for a branch
      in a tree
             overlooking the prison yard.
What he cranes to see
I manage to avoid:
      a fight, folding table, playing cards,
          someone's father.
The visiting room: smaller, yellower
      than the world outside.
In winter,
ducks gather
      in the watery part of the pond,
ice crystals forming   inches from feather.

    Tell me how a body can be both
              soft and hard—
if my dog will ever quit licking his bowl
once all the food disappears
      or if he's doomed to try
          and try again—
why I hesitate to explain
      even to my love
that I sometimes pray seated on the toilet—
no making a show of my need,
      instead
          tugging at a question mark,
touching one palm to the other,
      imagining a shovel,
and then the hole,   wide and deep.

Summer Solstice

The doorbell rang
                (or did they knock?),

then a cavalcade of shoes
                & eyes & teeth on the stairs;
their badges—everything—glinting.

The heavy footfalls
shook my wooden Barbie mansion

& toppled Power Rangers
in line at the McDonald's drive-thru

as they snaked right
                to his basement office,

only roots & stems visible
in our flower boxes above—

Not this again.
                Can't I pick a different lock?

Summer solstice brings out
the horror movie in me,

the Capture the Flag in me,
the junior high cartwheel in me.

A series of things followed by
a series of things.

I keep my mind razor sharp
in case of intruder, & some mornings

I stick a fork in a memory
& it comes out clean.

Mavis Beacon Teaches Typing

Soothing voiceover instructions still can't make my fingers
jab with grace like Mavis's expert hands at work.

I passed the end section exams by moving my thumbs
and index fingers quickly, the way a crab claws at algae.

Now slow hands are punctuated by fast fingers.
I misspell everything,

search results free of rule, a series of sparks and shapes tethered
to something wordless, which Mavis left for me to find.

A group of crabs is called a cast, and once when I was on a beach,
a single digit, I turned toward the water and there they were,

dozens of them, still as sand.

The One Where _____ _____

At 3am, I watch the episode of *Friends* where everyone's late to Thanksgiving dinner. I think about my father, the missing letters he wrote me. I never asked him what they eat in prison on Thanksgiving— if there are _____, if the _____ are mashed; if there are _____, if the _____ are canned. And the knives: where they're kept, if they go missing, what happens if they go missing. Same goes for forks, spatulas, tongs, spoons. Anything can be _____, brought outside or back to a cell and used to _____ someone. But the day a man broke my father's _____, he used his hands.

I fixated. I still do. The day I visited the prison in Ohio where they shot _____, I took photos of the rows—so many rows—of cells. A green-gray panorama. When I reached the "_____," I chose one and stood inside. Closed the door—a single slit so narrow all I could make out was the idea of bodies moving past. Light: no body. Dark: body. Unseen knowns: tourists flashing their cameras; their _____ shirts, fanny packs, _____ hats; their headphones; young children; _____. The echo of their laughter inside my _____, and inside my _____. My father spent an entire _____ in one of these. Just his hands and the idea of their shape, not their shape.

Tzitzit

On the bottom shelf of the dark bookcase, inside a velvet bag:
my father's tallit, white with blue, still perfect
after years free from dust—mailed to me the winter
my grandmother died. Its careful embroidery I cannot read,

turn each letter over in my mind, feel for its shape—
an alphabet lost when I was young.
I never became a bat mitzvah.

Her porcelain geese (or are they swans?) line my shelves;
I keep her heavy blue-green bowl on the floor,
an empty urn. I don't know where it lived when it was hers.
How to imagine or reconcile the shape of her face

in those last years, my yellowed school photos on her fridge.
That year they sent a photo album; I am five, six, never older
than eleven, and she is eternally grandmother-aged.

Enormous eyeglasses, fat pearl baubles hang from her ears
and neck—I touch them without care, as if they belong
only to me. Her locket knocks against my chest, now
I wear her ring. I kiss the tallit's fringe without its blessing.

Hive Mind

When caught in conversation
      my grandfather knew to say

he'd been talking only to himself

The visitors entered and spoke
      at once without warning

and one bright morning
      he boiled water in a pot

held it just above
      his daughter's head

humming

inside voices
      turned all the way up

Even after his death
      my grandmother called it stress

On Violence

Forbidden breakfast in my childhood home:
a forkful of funfetti cake

inches from my mouth & my father rounding the corner,
me about to cause his episode—

or maybe it was returning from a commercial break,
a rerun so frequent I forget the details. Years later,

I didn't have words for the woman who smacked her dog in the park
so hard

I felt it redden my cheeks from my hiding spot behind the trees,
the leash in my hand gone slack, the two of us stalled—

this the wilderness, the same wilds blooming within me
as on the morning security confiscated my knife at the airport,

my face warm and damp as I begged for it back,
anger simmering,

beneath it, ice melting,
because someone I love gave me that knife for Christmas,

the wrapping so plain and precise
I felt the edge of safety before I saw it.

Vitrine

[1]

The black & white queens
from a chess set, marble, sold years ago.

[2]

My dead grandmother
& her three porcelain geese, palm sized.

[3]

A clay hummingbird lost to time—
potted in a planter with hanging flowers,

fake. I molded, fired, & hid him myself;
he never fluttered out.

[4]

The sapphire he gave me,
under glass, in a drawer—for someday,

for something;

the fact of it unusual, blue, & fragile—
& somehow still true.

Transcription Beta (low confidence)

I'm calling from your mistakes,
reads the voicemail transcript
& I believe it.

♦ ♦ ♦

The MetroCard Machine Asks Whether I Want to Add Value or Time

a question I can't answer
when I'm already late, waxing optimistic
about my father's weekly meetings.

Hell is the visiting room and its cheap piano,
its dime-store books,
its dime-thin adolescent girls, an old woman
who berates a grown son for coming,

and my father, still drugged,
with the pebbled skin of someone
washed up on land.

I have seen his wife hold his face
in her hands, eyes closed,
moving her mouth without sound,
praying to a god I'd let go.

I've been praying to ghosts
because they seem more likely to listen,
all air and exorcism.

I've believed in wilder things,
like palm readers, trains that run on time,
a heaven I can touch:

my dog on the couch,
his warm body crushed against mine—
after the cops, after the quiet, softly snoring
to break the silence.

Passing Through East Harlem

cab window cracked,
there's a little dog sniffing the sidewalk for crumbs, collarless.

Ribs show through its blonde fur, tufts of it—
maybe six months old. You ask aloud what you should do

when what you want to do is jerk the handle and go,
but the person beside you in the backseat warns against it, says

you don't have gloves, you have to keep going, sure
there's a number you can call though he doesn't know it. You dial

311 instead of 911—correct, the operator says,
as does the next, and the next,

until you reach a dispatcher who notes the intersection,
the dog's slight build, its color, a shock of yellow

superimposed on a beige city block.
But she can't say whether a driver will reach the dog, corral it—

how it works, if ever it does,
if they use a net or treats, or a whistle, whether the shelter is kill

or no kill—
she only thanks you and hangs up, surrendering you to Saturday.

Cosign

The young paralegal says
he wouldn't wish this on anyone;

I can't feel the weight of the phone in my hand
or my hand,
            only their soft edges;

were I anyone,
instead of stone-faced at my desk,
staring out the window at a pond

around which dead trees strain to come back to life;

February 14th,
I can't find my father's keyboard—

just the set of small prisms he gave me
when he left for prison.
Five crystalline shapes in a locked box.

            Years later, a new trial.

More is required this time—
my signature for his bail bond.

            I sit on the floor with my dog,
stroke his ears while he sleeps;
loss happens so much slower than I used to think.

Not writing my name on a line is a cliff dive, an ellipsis
that feels like a period from which there is
no return.

Handheld

There's another version of this story
where I drain the past, rouge my cheeks
with its blood, make a dead thing live.

But in this one, I stole things.
Some wants are wanton—
you only know it

once it's in your pocket.
That's why I did what I did that day,
after recess ended & I stayed put,

dug up a Tamagotchi in the sand
below the monkey bars—
pixelated pet lost beside the blacktop.

Covered it with my hand,
slid it into my pocket, later
pushed its buttons, tried to revive it.

I couldn't. & that afternoon
I sat in my closet
until the sun went down,

listened for the silver bell of your voice,
pushed back plastic hangers
weighed down with sweaters,

& climbed out.

Maybe Five Years

my attorney says
maybe five years

I am reading
        these words
from my father

as if
under crush of waves

my fingers bobbing
for air

        oh let me up

summer sun
scorching the earth

        or let me
stay down here

if I am not to be
        released

I hear the operator
above & below

or memory of her
        tinkling voice

asking if I will accept
the charges

seakelp dredged
in my mouth

Visitor to Ice Canyon

The cheaper brand of water bottle,
label cartoonish on the nightstand:

Ice Canyon the only unreal place
from which I've ever drunk.

Poland Spring has nothing
on Ice Canyon,

which tastes like a fairytale brook
cut with hand soap.

And which you bought for us
at the all-night CVS

where some man,
you said, dripped blood

down the aisles
and the checkout line.

That's a lot of blood,
is all I thought in the moment,

watching you uncap the bottle
with your perfect, clean hands.

Party Cops

The man three cubicles away keeps clearing his throat

        making relief sounds like   *ah*   and   *whew*

& I am seconds from my next great line but it slips past

        something something

yes   a line about the call I took yesterday

        with the forensic psychologist about my father

how when I thanked her for calling   I meant it

        there's a poem there

I mean   maybe there's a poem there

        but that poem is somewhere hidden from me

& I get to thinking instead

           about the man at Starbucks this morning

        who lapped the store repeating words

then paused at my table

        said something about a party & the cops

           (like that's where his time stopped)—

party cops   clear as day

        though the last clear day was Monday

& it hasn't been Monday for days

Disappearing Act

The day god went missing again,
we made cake from cornmeal and sea salt,
yellow grit sticking to our palms
like a psalm felt instead of read.
I can't overhear another statistic
about the prison system
because all I see is my father in his cell,
khaki drab and tunnel vision.
I wanted him here in our home state,
a dark North Star
guiding me home in the black web of trains
I ride underground in a city he can't stand.
It's too loud, too cold, too full of people
who don't pay attention,
refused him the fame he sought.
Once he asked why I left San Francisco—
clear ocean, 90-degree hills, better burritos;
I couldn't tell him there were nephews,
how I missed
the jangle of my mother's bracelets,
the feeling I get now when the plane lands
and I am back in New York,
where they don't see me
if I don't want to be seen,
because home is an abstraction,
like sheet music without a sheet,
and my calculator doesn't do long division
but I know it's been years
since we plucked guitar strings
at his house with its wind chimes,
its sliding back door, all his breakable things.

Jiordan Castle is a writer and brand strategist from Long Island, New York. She received her BA in English from the University of San Francisco and her MFA in Poetry from Hunter College. Winner of the 2018 *Pigeon Pages* essay contest, her work has appeared in various online journals and print magazines. She lives in New York City with a pug named Hacksaw. You can find her at jiordancastle.com and @jiordancastle everywhere else.

CPSIA information can be obtained
at www.ICGtesting.com
Printed in the USA
BVHW030046220120
569913BV00002B/66